Internet and Technology Dangers

The Wake Up Call Every Parent Needs

Steve W Roche

Published by Dragonwood
First Published 2012

Internet and Technology Dangers

ISBN 978-0-9546805-9-6

Design by Sparkwave – **www.sparkwave.co.uk**

For more information:

InternetDangers
SHOWING YOU HOW TO SURF SAFELY

www.internetdangers.com

Protechtion

www.protechtion.org.uk

Dragonwood
Publishers

www.dragonwood.co.uk

This book is dedicated to my wonderful mum who so sadly died in 2003 and my lovely wife, Dominica, the caring and loving mother of our son, Mark.

INTERNET AND TECHNOLOGY DANGERS

Contents

INTRODUCTION

This Is Your Wake Up Call

"The Internet is an uncharted world. It's a world that parents don't know, but kids do. Parents would be shocked to see what goes on."

Detective Chris Loyko of a Cyber Crimes Investigations Unit in Florida

These days most children and young people know about the dangers associated with the Internet, mobile phones and video games. Safety lessons are now taught at most schools. But too many youngsters ignore the warnings and still take risks.

But, as a parent, how much do you know about Internet and technology dangers? As a parent, you can't help worrying about your children. You may be concerned about them:

- getting into the wrong company;
- being bullied;
- getting into trouble with the authorities;
- growing up too quickly;
- coming to emotional harm; or
- being sexually exploited.

Did you know that any of these things is a risk anytime your child uses the Internet? Something could be happening right now.

This book is intended as your wake up call. Its purpose is actually to alarm you. I don't want you to panic, but I do want you to act. After all, the emotional and physical wellbeing of your family is at stake here.

The dangers which are discussed in this book are not being taken seriously enough by parents, children or society as a whole. Putting your head in the sand is not an option. Ignoring the problem won't make it go away. The Internet, mobile phones and video games are here to stay. So simply barring children from using technology won't work.

When it comes to the dangers posed by the Internet, mobile phones or video games, we seem to read or hear about a new scare every day in the media. But most parents don't do anything as a consequence to protect their loved ones. Many parents feel powerless and fearful. Children and teenagers know more than they do about the Internet, mobile phones and video games.

Just to repeat the point – as you read this book, you need to act on the suggestions made.

What are the Internet and technology dangers?

The Internet, mobile phones and video games are rightly very popular with children and young people. They offer them a range of opportunities for fun, education and entertainment. But these technologies also open the door to many dangers.

For example:

- thanks to the Internet, it is now much easier for predators to reach and sexually exploit unsuspecting children;
- every child who goes online is just one click away from obscenely graphic and potentially addictive pornography; and
- a sinister form of bullying known as cyberbullying has grown rapidly in recent years.

The types of dangers are not necessarily new. But the Internet and gadgets bring the threats closer to home. Danger is a mouse click away. No child is safe from these risks. Many think they are, though. They think: "It'll never happen to me."

As a parent, you are the 'first line of defence' against online and technology dangers. Right here you'll acquire the knowledge, the confidence and the resources you need to protect your loved ones.

You'll find information about:

- what the dangers are;
- how big a risk they are;
- what you need to know about them; and
- what you can do to combat them and protect yourself and your family.

The main dangers relate to:

- pornographic, offensive and harmful websites
- online predators and child abuse
- social networking websites
- protecting your privacy
- cyberbullying
- technology addictions
- scams and commercial exploitation
- malware and hackers
- breaking the law
- mobile phones
- video games

When it comes to safety, what makes the Internet and new technologies different?

The first thing to understand is that the Internet and gaming cannot be made completely safe. There is no single point of control with the Internet. This makes it different from any other technology. Inevitably, children will come into contact with potential dangers.

Generally speaking, the risks are the same as real-world dangers. For example, bullying amongst teenagers has always been a problem.

The big difference is that the **problems are larger in scale and are heightened.** This is because of the nature of the Internet itself. For example, the perpetrators of online crimes can, up to a point, remain anonymous.

Take cyberbullying to illustrate the point. It can be more damaging than ordinary playground bullying.

One reason is that it can be difficult for a child to escape from it. A cyberbully can continue to bully their victim even when they're at home. The bully can reach them via their mobile phone or through email and instant messaging.

Research reveals that **people sometimes act differently on the Internet.** This is one of the main problems. Plus, they think they can avoid the consequences of what they say and do because they can bully **anonymously**.

Also because online conversations are not always in real-time or face-to-face, people don't get visual feedback on what they say as they say it. So they say and act in a more cruel way. This is more of an issue for children and teenagers. Many are still working out the social rules and don't yet have fully formed 'critical evaluation skills'.

The virtual lives of teenagers

A 2011 survey of the online activities of 2,300 young people aged between 11 and 18 from across the UK for the children's charity Kidscape, found that 45% of children are often happier with their online lives than they are with reality.

Many said that they feel that they can be exactly who they want to be online. Many also said that one of the things they like about the Internet is the control it gives them. For example, as soon as something they are doing online is no longer fun, they can simply hit the quit button.

Other findings from the survey

- 1 in 8 teenagers are in contact with strangers when on the web and often lie about their appearance, their age and their background.
- 47 per cent of children said they behave differently online than they do in their normal lives. Many claimed it makes them feel more powerful and confident.

"These findings suggest that children see cyberspace as detachable from the real world and a place where they explore parts of their behaviour and personality that they possibly would not show in real life. We can't allow cyberworlds to be happier places than our real communities, otherwise we are creating a generation of teenagers not functioning adequately in our society."

Peter Bradley, Deputy Director of the UK Charity, *Kidscape*

We're Not Taking This Problem Seriously Enough

Worrying Statistics

Cyberbullying

In a study conducted by the University of London in July 2006:

- over 1 in 5 of teenagers said that they had been cyberbullied at least once; and
- almost 7% said they had been cyberbullied more often.

Offensive websites

34% of teenagers report they have "received unwanted exposures to sexual material." According to research, the more times people see offensive material, the more desensitised they become to it. They begin to regard it as normal. Offensive material can have a negative impact on a child's self-esteem.

Online predators

A US Congressional study found that:

- 1 out of 5 teenagers have been solicited for sex on the Internet;
- an estimated 725,000 American children have been aggressively pursued for sex on the Internet; and
- 1 out of 4 children have been sent pictures of people who were naked or who were taking part in sexual activity.

A University of New Hampshire Crimes Against Children Research Center study found that one in seven (13%) teenagers had received "unwanted sexual solicitations or approaches in the past year".

The survey also found that:

- 43% of the sexual solicitations were from teenagers under the age of 18; and
- 14% of the pursuers were people the victims already knew.

Other interesting findings from this study are listed below.

- Offenders rarely used deceit or violence. Instead, they appealed to the natural interest of teenagers in romance and sex.
- 66% handled unwanted approaches by removing themselves from the situation:
    - by blocking the pursuer;
    - leaving the website;
    - or by switching off their computer.
- Others told the person to stop, confronted or warned the pursuer (16%), while some ignored them (11%).

- Most victims didn't report the incidents to their parents or authorities.
    - Only 5% of the incidents were referred to the police.
    - 12% said they reported it to their parents.
    - Just 2% reported it to teachers or the school.
    - In more than half of cases (56%) the teenagers did not tell anyone about the solicitations.

Online pornography

The same University of New Hampshire Crimes Against Children Research Center study found that exposure to unwanted porn is a large and growing problem.

In the study:

- 34% of teenagers reported they have "received unwanted exposures to sexual material";
- 92% removed themselves from the situation; and
- only 2% of the teenagers who came across sexual material said they went back to that site later.

Privacy invasions

- 75% of children are willing to give personal information in exchange for goods or services.

Technology addiction

- Research shows that because the Internet and gadgets are fun activities they place greater demands on our self-control. This can then lead to addiction.

- People can get a 'dopamine buzz' from using these technologies. The brain's 'natural reward pathway' can get hijacked.

Video games

- Themes that are sometimes depicted include graphic violence, sexual scenes, drug taking, drinking alcohol, propaganda and bad language.
- Only "17% of children say their parents check the ratings on the video games they buy".

"We were alarmed by the number of risks being taken by teenagers whilst online. Safe online behaviour is taught in schools, but teenagers seem to be unable to relate the risks to themselves. This research should challenge teenagers, parents and professionals to do their best to make internet safety guidelines meaningful."

Peter Bradley, Deputy Director of the UK Charity, *Kidscape*

You Are The First Line Of Defence

Emotions can run high when talking about these issues. Organisations and people get blamed for the problems. In the short-term, though, it's best if we, as parents, focus on doing the things which are within our control. This includes, for example:

- getting our children to the stage where they are able to manage the risks they face themselves; and
- doing what we can as adults to make their digital experiences safer.

There is a generational divide, though. Many parents do not necessarily feel equipped to help their children in this area. Many parents, therefore, feel fearful but helpless.

The situation is not helped by the fact that children and young people are growing up in what is being called a 'risk averse' culture. They spend more time indoors than previous generations did. But to develop as people, they need to take risks and to learn to socialise. So what they do is meet these needs on the Internet and by playing video games.

Although they are confident with the technology, they still haven't developed their 'critical evaluation skills'. This is why they need the help of parents to make wise decisions when it comes to technology.

The fact is that a child can only get the full benefits of the Internet by also running up against the potential risks. But many parents either underestimate or don't realise how often children and young people come across potentially harmful and inappropriate material on the Internet.

Everyone needs to be involved in fixing these problems. This includes families, industry, government and others. But, as a parent, you are where it needs to start for your children.

Action needs to be taken in three areas.

- The availability of potentially harmful material needs to be reduced. This is a job for the Internet, mobile phone and video games industries along with governments.
- Access to harmful material needs to restricted. This is a job for parents and everyone else involved in the care of children.
- The resilience of children needs to be developed. Again that this is a job for parents and everyone else involved in the care of children.

Children and teenagers need to be 'helped to help themselves' when it comes to safety. Children will be children. They push boundaries and take risks.

The threats posed by Internet and technology dangers are no different to any other child safety issue.

Take road safety, for example. Crossing the road can be dangerous, so how do we tackle the problem? The authorities put up barriers in dangerous locations and place road safety signs where they can be seen. They also employ people to help young children cross the road on their way to and on their way home from school.

Parents also teach children how to cross the road. Importantly, the teaching is done in stages.

1. We start by getting them to hold our hands when they cross the road.

2. Then we teach them how to cross the road but we continue to carry on crossing the road with them and holding their hand.
3. Later, when we see that they are starting to understand, we let them cross the road without holding our hand but we make sure they walk beside us.
4. Eventually we let them cross on their own but with us watching from a distance.
5. Then finally we let them cross the road on their own without any supervision.

Going online and playing video games may be a more complicated process than crossing the road, but the same principles apply. As a parent you should change your approach as your child becomes less vulnerable, more streetwise and more competent.

This is the 21st century parenting skill

Unfortunately, no child is safe. Children from all backgrounds and of all ages face risks. So you need to teach yourself, and then your family, how to avoid the dangerous aspects of the Internet, mobile phones and video games.

You need to show children how to deal with the dangers when, and not if, they come into contact with them. So teaching resilience is also therefore very important. It is the ability to bounce back from a trauma or adversity.

Ways that you can teach children to become resilient include:

- trying to talk openly and honestly with them about things which are appropriate for their age;
- making the family home an emotionally safe place;

- limiting the amount of time they are exposed to television, newspapers and the media in general;
- helping them to understand that there is a link between stress and moods;
- establishing routines for things such as bedtime and doing jobs around the house;
- teaching them how to express their fears; and
- teaching them how to develop a positive outlook on life.

Different ages, different dangers

- Cyberbullying is the most common risk that junior school age children face.
- Privacy problems and reputation protection are the biggest issues that secondary school and university students face.

Different ages, different approaches

Parents tend to have more control over children under the age of 12 than they do over teenage kids. The young ones need more guidance and supervision.

Teenagers are just as at risk as younger children even though they're older and perhaps more streetwise.

It is important to bear in mind that teens are:

- more independent;
- less likely to listen to warnings from adults;
- more influenced by their peers than by their parents;
- naturally curious;
- inclined to push boundaries and take risks;

- often think they know best;
- more likely to use the Internet to seek out relationships:
- far more likely to meet up with someone they've met online; and
- more likely to be taken in by commercial exploitation.

Research shows that teenagers:

- welcome more freedom;
- want more understanding from parents; and
- should be listened to so that they feel what they think is important.

Actions you can take

Look for the warning signs

Here some possible pointers that there may be something to be concerned about when it comes Internet dangers.

- Changes in the behaviour of your child. Perhaps they're trying to hide something from you related to what they're doing online.

- Spending too much time on the Internet, particularly at night. This could be a signal that they're talking to strangers online or that they're becoming addicted.

- Spending time in chat rooms, especially unmoderated ones – these are ones where there is no supervision.

- Downloading image files – these are computer files with names ending in the letters .jpg, .gif, .bmp, .tif and .pcx.

- Receiving phone calls from strangers.

Your job as a parent

Here are 14 general things you should do.

1. Get the necessary technology skills.
2. Learn the jargon.
3. Be cautions and alert to the possible dangers. But keep a proper sense of perspective.
4. Teach your children critical thinking skills and resilience.
5. Be sensible. For example, in the same way that you'd ask your teenage kids where they were going to if they were going out for the evening and who they were going with, make sure you ask what sites they are visiting and who they are meeting there.
6. Be constructive. Lecturing, spying, and banning Internet access will not work.
7. As you will learn later in this book, you should be as concerned about what your children say while online as what they see.
8. Don't just focus on the dangers which receive all the media coverage such as online pornography and predators. There are other risks ranging from cyberbullying through to addiction and scams that you need to be aware of.
9. If children do open up to you about bad experiences on the Internet, don't overreact or blame them. Listen carefully. Welcome the fact that they have told you about their troubles.
10. Be hands-on and involved with your children when it comes to the Internet and the tech gadgets they use.
11. PCs are better than laptops for children. Locate the computer in a family room where you can see it. It's not a good idea for it to be tucked away in a bedroom.

12. Listen and learn. Find out from your child what they use the computer for and how they use the Internet.
13. Be understanding. Remember what it was like when you were their age.
14. Remember that, while children need a certain amount of privacy, they also need parents to be involved in this aspect of their daily lives.

Set groundrules

- As a parent, you know only too well that if you tell a child not to do something then, the chances are, they will. So be prepared to negotiate at times.
- Show them why you're setting rules. It's a good idea to help children see for themselves how they might get into difficulties if they don't do as you say.
- How you present your safety rules is important. You'll probably find that they'll respond more positively if you represent things as a way for them to be 'cool' on the Internet.
- Post the rules you mutually agree near the computer as a reminder.
- Monitor how well they stick to the rules.

Install Internet Security Software

If it's not already set up on your computer, you should get Internet Security software. New computers typically now have trial versions pre-installed from companies such as Norton and McAfee.

Most Internet Security software these days comes with a feature known as Parental Control. Consider setting it to 'on'.

Typical parental control features are:

- control over the websites and content that can be viewed;
- control over what can be downloaded and installed; and
- regulation of the times the computer can be used.

Above all, you need to get home the message that they could become a victim.

DANGER 1

Pornographic, offensive and harmful websites

It's worrying that very depraved material is just a few clicks away from any child who goes online. Either deliberately or by accident, children can come across distressing material such as:

- extreme pornography;
- violent images; and
- propaganda, hate and cult websites.

Pornographic websites

Be warned

These days teenagers are being exposed to an almost constant stream of sexually charged images from the Internet and the traditional media like TV, newspapers and magazines.

The more often a person is exposed to these things, the more normal it seems and the more desensitised they become. These things can have an enormous impact on a child's self-esteem and potentially his or her future.

Problems associated with the exposure to pornography

Research has been done which indicates that the widespread availability of pornography increases the threat of children becoming victims of sexual violence.

There is also said to be a link between pornography and incidents of rape and sexual violence. Furthermore, there is evidence of a link between pornography and child molestation.

Research has been conducted which reports that widespread exposure to pornography for children:

- frequently results in unplanned pregnancies, sexual illnesses and sexual addiction later in life;
- may incite children to play out sexual acts against other children;
- shapes attitudes and values; and
- interferes with a child's development and identity.

The Internet is saturated with pornography. Extraordinarily explicit images are one click away from the eyes of vulnerable children.

With all this exposure to porn, the question that is increasingly being asked is whether teenagers are becoming negatively affected by online porn. Or are they sensible enough to see through it?

For some children, all that they know about sex is coming from explicit websites. Their heads are being filled with an assortment of sexual fantasies and scenarios. So much so, that when it comes to making love to a real person many have no idea how to behave. It seems that a whole generation of teenagers is being contaminated by Internet porn before they ever have the chance to have sex for real or enjoy a genuine relationship with a person from the opposite sex.

As adults, do we not have a responsibility to protect the next generation from the implications of this?

Worrying statistics

- A third of ten year olds have viewed pornography on the Internet.

- Four out of every five children aged 14 to 16 admit to regularly looking at explicit photographs and videos on their home computers.
- One in every four clicks on the Internet is related to porn.
- Every second 28,258 Internet users are viewing porn.
- There are 420 million pornographic webpages on the Internet.
- The average age that children first get exposed to pornography is 11.
- 90% of children aged 8 – 16 have viewed porn online.

Propaganda, hate and cult websites

Racist and terrorist groups are using the Internet to:

- recruit new members; and
- spread their propaganda.

Disturbingly, many hate websites go out of their way to attract children. They know that children and young people are impressionable so they specifically target them with unpleasant messages. Some hate sites have dedicated children's sections with music, puzzles and other features that kids go for.

Children can stumble across offensive websites by accident.

- For example, sometimes by typing quite innocent words into a search engine they can be taken to websites that contain offensive material. The operators try to get their sites to appear on search engine results pages for search phrases such as the names of popular cartoon characters and famous pop stars.

- Another approach they sometimes take to trick people onto their sites is buying and using website names that are very similar to those of well-known companies. This is called typosquatting.
- A third way is via unsolicited emails (known as spam). Often spam emails contain offensive pictures and links to pornographic websites.

What to do if you're worried

- Check the 'safe search' setting of the search engine you are using. Google has three settings – off, moderate and strict.
- Microsoft's search engine, Bing, has the same three settings. To change them, you click on the Preferences option from the home page.
- Report any offensive material that you or your children come across. You'll find details of the organisations that you can report offensive material to at Appendix 2.

Pro-suicide websites

There are pro-suicide sites on the Internet which encourage people to take their own lives and offer advice on how to do it.

The number of people who are killing themselves in suicide pacts arranged over the Internet is a concern. 29 'Internet suicides' were uncovered in Britain between 2001 and 2008.

Search engine companies and Internet Service Providers say they cannot block access to pro-suicide websites unless they are made illegal by the Government.

What to do if you're worried

The UK suicide charity, Papyrus, offer the following advice on how to deal with someone if you think they may be considering suicide.

- Show an interest. Try to find out their real problems.
- Don't hesitate to bring up the subject of suicide. Talking about it will not make things worse.
- Do not condemn suicide websites outright. Give reasons why they are not the best way of finding information and getting support.
- Explain that pro-suicide websites and chat rooms only provide one option. They do not offer alternatives such as medication, therapy or support from family and friends.
- Make sure they know that many people have suicidal feelings but can and do overcome them to live normal lives.
- Suggest alternative websites that can offer positive support.
- Listen to what they tell you and do not be judgmental.
- Tell them that you love them no matter what and give them a hug.
- If they won't talk to you, encourage them to talk to a friend or sibling.
- If they are living away from home, go and see them.

Sources of help in the UK

- **Papyrus**
  0870 170 4000
  www.papyrus-uk.org

- **The Samaritans**
  08457 909090
  www.samaritans.org

Advice sites

There are a number of very dubious advice sites around covering topics such as:

- pro-anorexia;
- self-harm; and
- drugs and alcohol.

What to do if you're worried

Speak to your children and make the following points.

- Be very careful about taking advice from websites. Unless there's a section telling you who runs the site and what their expertise is, they may not be qualified to offer advice no matter how well-intentioned they may be.

- Don't take any medical advice from a website.

DANGER 2

Online predators and child abuse

"Predators will look for any way to talk to children online whether through sites like MySpace, instant messaging, or even online games."

Mike Fitzpatrick, US Congressman

Be warned

Children use Internet chat rooms and social networking sites such as Facebook a lot. Girls, in particular, use the Internet to stay in touch and to socialise with their friends.

Predators know this and so hang out on the same websites. They use the Internet to make contact with children and teenagers. They are on the lookout for children they can target. Their aims can include abduction or sexual abuse. Sometimes the aim is to get a child involved in criminal activity.

Child pornography is another major problem. So, at times, the aim may be to persuade a child to provide an indecent picture of themselves.

Worrying statistics

One estimate is that there are over 100,000 separate websites around the world which contain images of children being abused.

In 2008, BBC TV's Panorama programme commissioned a survey of more than 800 parents and youngsters. The aim was to find out:

- how teenagers use the Internet; and
- what their parents knew about that use.

The survey found that there is a difference between what parents think their children do online, and what they actually do.

The survey found that:

- 25% of the children had given out personal details such as a name or mobile number on the Internet. Only 13% of parents thought their children had done this.
- 15% of children admitted to chatting to strangers online. Only 10% of parents thought their children had done this.

A study by the UK's Child Exploitation and Online Protection Centre (CEOP) found that 25% of children said that they had met up face-to-face with someone they first met on the Internet.

What is online child abuse?

There are two basic types.

- Where someone makes or downloads images of children being sexually abused.
- Where someone goes online and approaches a child for sex. This could be either:
    - **online sex** – for example, sexual activity using texting or a webcam; or
    - **offline sex** – for example, grooming a child online for the purpose of meeting up for sex in the "real" world.

The problem of child pornography

- Many paedophiles admit that seeing images of child sex on the Internet fuels their fantasies. Many have confessed that the online child pornography they have seen has played an important part in leading them to commit physical sexual offences against children.

- This is a very serious problem because, according to the children's charity NCH, the demand for child pornography on the Internet is growing and has led to an increase in sex abuse cases.
- People interested in child pornography can get hold of images by paying to subscribe to websites that deal in that kind of material.
- More worryingly, they can get hold of pictures for nothing and anonymously by using what is called 'peer-to-peer file -sharing software'.

Most mobile phones these days have built-in cameras and camcorders. This makes the problem worse.

How paedophiles operate on the Internet

We know that paedophiles use specific methods to:

- find their potential victims; and
- to 'groom' the children they find that match their preferences.

What is grooming?

The official definition of grooming is:

A course of conduct enacted by a suspected paedophile, which would give a reasonable person cause for concern that any meeting with a child arising from the conduct would be for unlawful purposes.

In other words, it's the process that paedophiles use to get children they find on the Internet to meet them face-to-face in order to carry out sexual abuse.

How paedophiles find their potential victims

- Predators try to meet children in places like Internet chat rooms and social networking sites such as Facebook.
- They start by looking at the profiles people create for themselves on these websites.
- The sort of information that people can include in their chat room or social networking profile is:
    - their real name;
    - their age;
    - where they live;
    - a photograph; and
    - their hobbies and interests.
- This kind of information is very valuable to a paedophile. It helps them find children who match what they're looking for as far as age, physical appearance and geography are concerned.
- Often a paedophile will try to persuade a child to add them as one of their friends. If a child agrees to this request, the paedophile is then able to make contact with all of that child's friends.
- If a paedophile knows about the hobbies and interests of a child, they are able to use that information in a sinister way. For example, they might send a hoax email pretending to be from an organisation that relates to a particular hobby or interest.

- Sometimes paedophiles provide a false description of themselves. For example, they might make out that they are a child of a particular age or gender in the hope that they'll attract the interest of a child of a similar type. Some paedophiles, though, state openly that they are adults.

A chat room conversation might start like this:

13/m/uk (This means "I am 13 years old, I am male and I am in the UK")

Then they'll wait for a child to respond.

Next they might vet the child or children that respond by asking a few questions.

Another approach they use is to enter the chat room and do nothing except watch the conversations that are taking place. When they spot a child that they like the sound of, they'll introduce themselves by sending a private message directly to that child.

The 5 stages of Internet grooming

Experts have identified a pattern that online predators work through as they attempt to groom a child.

Stage 1 – the friendship forming stage

- This is when the paedophile is getting to know the child.
- At this stage, paedophiles will sometimes ask if the child has a picture of themselves.
- They want to be sure that the person they are talking to actually is a child, and not someone posing as a child.

- They also want to check that the child matches the profile of the type of child they are looking for.
- The length of time spent at this stage varies.
- The paedophile will try and have these sorts of discussions in private rather than public areas of the website if they can.

Stage 2 – the relationship forming stage

- This is where the conversation gets more personal. The paedophile will try and get the child to talk about subjects such as school or their life at home.
- The paedophile is trying to create the impression that they are the child's friend.
- Some paedophiles do not take the conversation into this stage. Sometimes they will take the relationship to this stage but will mix in conversations that relate to the next stage of the grooming process.

Stage 3 – the risk assessment stage

- By this point the paedophile has decided that they are interested in the particular child. What they want to do next is to find out if it is safe to progress any further.
- So for example the paedophile might ask questions about the location of the computer the child is using and the number of other people who use it.

Stage 4 – the exclusivity stage

- If the paedophile is happy that they will go undetected then they will up the pace.
- They'll try to get the child to trust them. They might try to get the child to think that they are now best friends. Or they might try to get the child to understand that they know what they're going through.
- They'll try to get the child to regard their relationship as a secret that must always be kept that way.
- Often the paedophile will test this out by questioning how much the child trusts them.

Stage 5 – the sexual stage

- This is when the paedophile moves the conversation onto a more intimate level.
- Typically, they'll ask questions such as "Have you ever been kissed?" or "Do you ever touch yourself?"
- Often they'll say things like "You can talk to me about anything."
- At this stage there will be differences in the pattern of conversations depending on the motivation of the paedophile. For example, if they're looking for a relationship, they will enter the sexual stage gently.
- If the child seems uncomfortable, the paedophile will then express deep regret and will ask the child to forgive them.

- At this stage statements that the paedophile may make include: "Maybe we could meet some day and I could show you how much I love you". Or: "Maybe you could take some photographs of yourself?"
- Sometimes the paedophile will make suggestions and on other occasions they'll make explicit demands.
- The paedophile will often keep the focus of the conversation on the child. This is because they want to come across as a mentor who is guiding the child in certain ways.
- Sometimes things will be taken further. For example, the paedophile might tell the child that if they do the things suggested then they will become a wonderful lover.
- The research suggests that conversations of this type may progress to a request for a face-to-face meeting.
- During this stage it is common for the paedophile to instigate the exchanging of pornographic images.
- In doing this the paedophile might be seeking to justify their requests for the child to carry out sexual activities. They might also be hoping to lower the inhibitions of the child.
- The paedophile might then ask the child to take images or videos of him or herself that are similar to the images that have been exchanged.
- Ultimately, the paedophile may try to get the child to have 'cyber sex' with them by 'virtually' performing a sexual fantasy.

- Typically, they will start by describing a particular situation and then move on by inviting - or even blackmailing - the child to engage in cyber sex.
- Sometimes paedophiles carry out what is called 'cyber rape' because they use coercion, control and aggression to get the child to have 'cyber sex' with them.

Differences in the way that paedophiles operate

The motivation of the paedophile determines the process they use. For example, some paedophiles will remain in particular stages for longer than others. Sometimes stages are skipped.

What has been described here is a general pattern. Groomers will design what they say as they go along. They might tailor their flattery or offers as they learn about the victim.

The law

In the UK, the Sexual Offences Act makes 'Internet grooming' a specific offence. It is now illegal to arrange to meet a child with the intention of committing a sexual offence, even if sexual contact does not take place. The offence carries a sentence of up to seven years.

What to do if you're worried

Look for warning signs

How can you tell if your child is being groomed or abused online? The vast majority of children are not and never will be but you need to be vigilant nonetheless.

Your child might have quite legitimate reasons for:

- downloading files onto discs; or
- using encryption software.

But it is worth being curious as to why they're doing those sorts of things. Are they trying to hide something?

Look for changes in your child's behaviour. Such changes may be an indicator that something is going on. For example, look for:

- your child becoming secretive;
- a change in their level of self-esteem and self-confidence;
- your child withdrawing from the family and isolating themselves;
- your child having difficulties at school;
- your child becoming increasingly anxious;
- your child having sleeping difficulties;
- your child finding it difficult to concentrate; or
- your child becoming excessively concerned with washing and cleanliness.

What not to do

Don't ban your child from using the computer. That would be an over -reaction and can be counter-productive. One of the reasons why children don't open up about things is because they fear being banned from using the computer.

Never be tempted to carry out your own vigilante investigations to try to identify offenders. Doing so can:

- jeopardise police investigations;
- put you into a position where you may risk breaking the law yourself; and
- most importantly, can seriously endanger the safety of children.

Leave work of this kind to the professionals.

Speak to your children and make the following points.

- Never email or upload a photo of yourself or any of your friends to a website.
- Do not reveal too much personal information about yourself online. For example, never give out your phone number or the name of the school you go to.
- Never meet up with anyone who you meet online that you do not know.
- Only use chat rooms which are moderated.
- Do not tolerate anyone being rude or abusive to you while you are online. If this does happen then you should end the conversation and leave the site immediately.
- Never reply to nasty or suggestive messages or pictures. Tell an adult if you are sent any.
- Take care with webcams. Do not use them to send live video pictures.
- Look out for questions a predator might ask such as:
    - "Where's your computer in the house?"
    - "What's your favourite band/film?" This tells the predator about some of gifts they might offer.
    - "I know someone who can get you a modeling job." Predators often use flattery as a tactic.

    - "I know where you can get money fast."
    - "You seem sad, what's bothering you?" This is a ploy whereby the predator hopes to become a confidant.
    - "What's your phone number?"
    - "If you don't do what I ask I will …." Predators sometimes use threats of this kind.
- Make sure your mobile is protected with a security code.
- Make sure your mobile is never out of your sight.

DANGER 3

Social networking

Be warned

A question which is increasingly being asked is whether sites such as Facebook and Twitter are creating a generation of young people who are obsessed with themselves?

Some experts are beginning to believe that repeated exposures to social networking sites leave people with an identity crisis. They believe that some people are growing up with a need for instant gratification. There is also some evidence that people might be losing non-verbal communication skills such as the ability to make eye contact during conversations.

Some Facebook users feel the need to become 'mini celebrities' who crave being watched and admired by other people on a daily basis. Is a generation of people growing up thinking that the only thing that matters is what other people think about them?

Another side to the issue of social networking is the ease with which online predators can find victims using them. There have been cases where children have been abused by paedophiles that found and groomed them via their social networking pages.

Also, cyberbullies often use social networking sites to target their victims. Another risk is getting into trouble with friends or even the police by publishing inappropriate, offensive or illegal material on sites such as Facebook.

What is a social networking site?

Websites such as Facebook enable people to:

- build and stay in touch with friends and contacts;
- create an online place where they can showcase themselves and their interests; and
- express their identity and opinions.

The main social networking websites used by children and teenagers are Facebook, Bebo, and MySpace. They're all pretty similar in what they offer.

At the centre of things is what is called the profile. This is where you list details about yourself including your background, contact details and personal interests. You can also include photos on your profile.

You can use Facebook to communicate with friends and other users through private or public messages and a live chat feature. You can also create and join interest groups. Facebook enables people to choose their own privacy settings and to select who can see specific parts of their profile.

Talking to teenagers about their social networking

It is not easy discussing what they do on social networking sites with children and teenagers. They sometimes think of their social networking pages as their own private place. If you kept a private diary as a child, you'll know what this feels like.

Social networking sites are also a place where children meet and talk to their friends. Understandably, at times, they want those conversations to be private.

But this doesn't mean you shouldn't be involved in some way as a parent. After all, there have been many examples over the years of where children have got into difficulties because of what they've done and how they're behaved on sites such as Facebook.

So as a parent you need to strike a balance between educating them to behave safely on the one hand and trusting them to get on with it on the other.

Why teenagers social network

These days children live big parts of their lives online. They've grown up with the Internet. Consequently, they don't make as big a distinction as adults do between the 'online world' and the 'offline world'.

Sites such as Facebook and MySpace fit in really well with how they see the world. Social networking is a form of socialising, particularly for teenagers. They see sites such as Facebook as a way for them to express who they are.

So they regard spending hours each week finding and adding people to their network of friends as a perfectly natural thing to do. They read comments made by their friends on their profile and make comments on the profile pages of their friends.

Do you remember when you were young how important who your friends were, how your bedroom was decorated and what clothes you wore was to you? It was your way of expressing your identity and making a statement. Those things still matter to today's youngsters. But what also matters is how their social networking pages look and who their Facebook friends are.

Teenagers can use their social networking pages to say what they think. They can indicate their likes and dislikes and can join campaigns. They can join communities dedicated to things they enjoy such as music, hobbies and sports.

Teenagers see the Internet in a different way to how most adults do. For many adults the Internet is a way of finding things out or a convenient way to get things done like shopping. For teenagers, the Internet is much more than that. It's an extension of who they are.

Previous generations	This generation
Hung out with their friends outdoors.	Hang out with their friends indoors on the Internet.
Got their entertainment from the TV, radio and magazines.	Get their entertainment online. For example, YouTube and online radio stations.
Went to the library to do their homework.	Do their homework online.
Communicated using the telephone.	Communicate online using email, instant messaging and social networking sites.
Stored their stuff in their bedroom.	Store their stuff online digitally.
Played games at home or in the park.	Play games online.

An insight into how youngsters think about and use social networking websites

Teenagers think of social networking as a great way to meet new people and share experiences.

Figuring out who you are is a big part of what happens during the adolescent years. For today's youngsters, social networking websites play a big part in that process.

They use social networking sites in a very particular way. Many adults wander aimlessly around. Youngsters know their way around. They normally head straight to their profile page to check for messages from friends. If they're really bored they might browse around or start searching.

Teenagers tend to 'multi-socialise'. This means that when they're socialising online they'll, for example, be making a comment on Facebook, having a conversation with a friend on Instant Messaging and sending a text on their phone – all at the same time.

They might use one social networking site as their online diary and another one for hanging out with friends.

What's different about social networking is that it's a very public form of socialising. Not every young person likes it. But they feel they have to do it. Some teenagers think that they'll have more control if they expose their lives online themselves than if they wait for someone else to do it for them.

Parents and social networking

When they first look at social networking sites many parents look at the pages of other users and worry that their children might be mixing with people they don't like the look of. There is, of course, some basis to that concern but the truth is that most teenagers co-exist with other users of the sites but don't necessarily mix with them. They tend to just socialise with a select group of people.

Fear is very important because it alerts us to danger. One of the most important things that happen during adolescence is that youngsters develop their ability to assess risks. Learning about dangers is something that teenagers need to do for themselves with the help of their parents.

Every generation of parents wishes they could eliminate all risk from the lives of their children. When we look back through history we see that every generation of teenagers has done things or faced circumstances that have made their parents fearful. For example:

- in the 1950s parents worried about the influence of rock 'n' roll;
- in the 1960s parents worried about drugs and the sexual revolution; and
- in the 1970s parents worried about whether their children would find work when they left school.

Social networking is one of today's fears for parents.

Social networking and predators

A parent's worst nightmare is that their child is physically abused or abducted. Statistically the chances of this happening from an online encounter are very remote. But that doesn't mean you shouldn't be wary. Profiles on social networking sites can provide an enormous amount of valuable information for predators.

Predators can be extremely manipulative. So it is important to make sure that youngsters are aware of how skillful these people are. Predators can also be very patient. They are often very prepared to take the time needed to groom their victims by paying compliments and offering an understanding shoulder to lean on. They'll also sometimes try intimidation as a tactic.

Research shows that some types of teenagers are particularly vulnerable. An example is teenagers who are very compliant. This is because they are more likely to be the opposite when they're online. This means being non-compliant and taking chances they wouldn't normally take such as entering into conversations with people they meet online. But when under the influence of a predator, such children often revert back to their compliant selves because that's what they're used to doing.

'Perfect kids' can also be a concern. Offline they can feel there are things they can't express. When online, though, they can break out of that mold. They get a certain level of excitement and a sense of danger from the experience. Predators know how to take advantage of these thoughts. What makes the situation worse is that parents tend not to worry so much. They think that if their children are doing well at school and in life generally that they'll be fine in all situations.

What to do if you're worried

- Keeping kids and teenagers safe isn't just about technology. It's about parenting. Common sense will help them far more than parental control software ever will.
- It may sound overly simplistic, but the best way to protect children and teenagers is to talk to them. Not only about risks but also about the positive things they do when they're online. It should be two-way communication. Listen to them and be supportive plus keep an open mind. Whatever happens, don't overreact. Keep a sense of perspective. Be reasonable. For example:
    - pulling the plug on children's Internet activities is rarely a good idea as the first response;
    - it's then too easy for them to 'go underground' and get on the Internet from locations other than the home.
- It's also about teenagers developing resilience. They need to learn to think for themselves so that they can protect themselves. Help them to develop critical thinking skills.
- Teach them the importance of being friendly online. Research shows that teenagers who are aggressive and rude online towards friends or strangers are at greater risk of becoming victims themselves.
- Try to get your children to share their social networking profiles and blogs with you. The ideal way to monitor your child's social networking activity is to visit often and to look around.
- Be aware that your child might sign up for a social networking site using a false name.

- Reporting misconduct.
    - If you come across a profile and see something you consider to be inappropriate you can report it to the social networking site.
- Forms of misconduct include:
    - spam;
    - users of the site who are under age;
    - cyberbullying; and
    - copyright violation.
- Reporting problems
    - If you're reporting what you believe to be a crime or what you believe to be a risk to life, property or safety you should contact the police as well.
    - In the UK, CEOP offer an Abuse Reporting service.
    - You can report the following to the Internet Watch Foundation:
        - content which involves the sexual abuse of a child; and
        - content which is criminally obscene or which incites racial hatred.

Advice you can pass onto your children if you're worried

Suggest that they:

- Be as anonymous as possible.
- Never give out their address or phone number.
- Think very carefully about publishing photos or videos. Avoid posting sexually suggestive pictures or videos.

- If people can post comments on your profile or blog, check them often. Don't respond to nasty or embarrassing comments. Delete them and, if possible, block offensive people from commenting in the future.
- Be honest about your age. If you're too young to sign up for a service do not lie about your age.
- Be yourself when you're online. Don't be pressured to be someone you aren't.
- Treat other people the way you'd want to be treated yourself.
- People who are nasty and aggressive online are at greater risk of being bullied or harassed themselves.
- New people you meet online may act nice because they're trying to get something – if they're flattering or sympathetic it may be that they're trying to manipulate you in order to get something.
- Don't talk about sex with strangers.
- Be wary when talking to people you don't know especially if the conversation gets onto subjects like sex or how you look. Don't lead them on.
- Be careful when using your mobile. All the advice offered here in relation to computers, applies to mobile phones.
- Be careful who you give your number to.
- Be careful how you use GPS and other technologies that can pinpoint your physical location.
- Remember that what you say in a chat room or in an instant messaging session is live. You can't take it back or delete it later.

DANGER 4

Protecting your privacy

Some experts claim that the concept of privacy as we have come to know it is dead. That's because anyone can now publish whatever they want about themselves using social media sites. They can also publish anything they want about other people. For example, you can reveal very private information about yourself, upload photos and videos, share news and voice your opinions on Facebook.

Facebook has been described as the autobiographical novel that we are all writing. We can now become the 'WikiLeakers' of our own lives. Two leading American psychologists, Jean Twenge and Keith Campbell, have described this phenomenon as "the narcissism epidemic". They claim the self-promotional madness is driven by our need to broadcast our uniqueness to the world.

So the Internet has changed from being something we *read* into something we *read and write*. This ability is obviously fun and useful but there is a downside. Publishing too much information about yourself can have unintended consequences. If personal information gets into the wrong hands it can be dangerous.

Be warned that information can very easily get into the wrong hands. You can put your personal security at risk by publishing certain types of information on the Internet. Being too open with your private details can also lead to you becoming a victim of identity theft.

Even if they know the risks some people kid themselves by saying, "It'll never happen to me." It can.

Keeping your emails and computer files private

Think carefully about the kind of things you include in emails that you send. For example:

- Do you ever send financial information such as your bank details in an email?
- Do you ever say things about other people in emails that you wouldn't want them to one day see? Think carefully before you send emails. Ask yourself what might happen if the email ever got into the wrong hands.

Permanently deleting your files

Deleting an email or a file from your computer doesn't mean it has disappeared completely. It is still there stored on the hard drive of your computer. All you have done is delete the link to that file or email.

You need to use special software to permanently delete all the files or a particular file from your computer. An example of such software is SafeErase (www.laplink.com/safeerase).

If you decide to sell your computer you should always use file erasion software. If you don't then the person who buys your computer might be able to get hold of all your old files and details of the websites you visited on your computer.

Keeping your information private

Sometimes you'll want to save files, photos or videos onto a USB stick, a CD or a DVD. These are easily lost. Sometimes you'll also want to save personal information or passwords onto your computer.

There are privacy software programs available that can help with these risks. One example is Steganos Privacy Suite (www.steganos.com). It locks and encrypts your files and emails. It also organises and manages your passwords and permanently 'shreds' your unwanted data.

Surfing anonymously

Did you know that some website operators install a bit of computer code called a cookie on your computer when you visit their site? A cookie enables a website operator to track what you do on their website. This is not necessarily a bad thing as it can be useful for you and for them as they can customise their website for you. However, some unscrupulous website operators can use tracking software such as cookies to display unwanted adverts on your computer.

Surfing the Internet while you are using public wireless networks is also a risk as data hackers can 'eavesdrop' on what you're doing online.

You can get software which makes you anonymous and protects what you do online from being intercepted. One example is Steganos Internet Anonym (www.steganos.com).

Password security

These days so many sites are password-protected. Keeping track of all your passwords can be a problem.

People are rightly concerned about hackers getting into their computers to get hold of their passwords. But the truth is that many people put the privacy of their passwords are more at risk by being careless in more basic ways.

The most common mistakes made are:

- choosing a password that is easy to guess;
- using the same password all the time; or
- allowing other people to know their passwords.

Children need to be especially careful about sharing their passwords with friends. That's because it's not unusual for children to fall out with each other. And it's increasingly common for disgruntled ex-friend's to take out cyber-revenge by getting into the websites they use and playing pranks.

Always choose 'strong' passwords

It's tempting to choose easy-to-remember passwords for websites. These are called 'weak' passwords. Because they are easy-to-remember, it means they're also easy to crack.

How would you feel if someone you know or a criminal were able to guess the passwords for the websites you use? It does happen particularly when it comes to websites that contain information that might be useful for a criminal.

Password guess attacks

Cyber-criminals have ways for cracking passwords. They are called password guess attacks. There are three types:

- intelligent guess attacks;
- dictionary attacks; and
- brute force attacks.

So the stronger your password, the less likely that it will be guessed. Here's how to set a strong password.

- Make the password at least 7 characters long.
- Avoid obvious 'dictionary' words.
- Pick a combination of letters and numbers that you will remember but other people are unlikely to guess. Make sure you spell the word by using a mixture of lower and upper case characters, though.

Also, if you feel that you must write all your passwords down somewhere then make sure you store them in a non-obvious place.

What to do if you're worried

Advice you can offer your children

Tell them to:

- never give details about themselves to anyone they meet online who they don't know;
- never tell anyone their passwords;
- make sure other people do not watch over their shoulder when they login to their websites; and
- check with you first before providing information to a website, even if it's a well-known one.

Advice for you as a parent

Facebook

- Take care when you use sites such as Facebook. Why allow people you don't know that well to know what you're up to?
- Make sure you check your privacy settings. Check them regularly and make sure you know what all the settings mean.

Privacy policies

Always check for a privacy policy on the websites that your children use. Take the time to carefully read the policy if there is one. Find out:

- what personal information the website asks for; and
- how they say they'll use that information.

If you are at all concerned then don't let your child use the website. If the website doesn't publish a privacy policy then you should seriously consider whether your child should use it at all.

Think about installing a filtering software program onto your computer. This will make sure that information which you don't want you child to be able to send over the Internet such as their name, address or telephone cannot be sent.

Shopping online

Don't provide your credit or debit card details unless you're sure that the website you're buying from is secure. There is an easy way you can tell. When you get to the checkout page of the site, look at the first few letters of the website address.

- If it is secure, the letters 'https' will appear at the start before the 'www' part of the website address.
- If it is not secure, the first few letters will be 'http'.

The 's' signifies after 'http' tells you that it is a secure checkout system and your credit card details will be sent in a scrambled (encrypted) format over the Internet from your computer to the website you're buying from.

Protecting your reputation

More and more often these days you'll find that universities and employers are carrying out background checks on candidates by checking social media websites, personal blogs and videosharing websites such as YouTube.

So the question that children and teenagers need to ask before they publish comments, photos or videos of themselves on the web is: "Would I want a university I might apply to join or a future employer seeing this?"

Once content is published on the Internet, it can be difficult 'taking it back' later. Facebook does let you delete posts. But by the time you get around to doing that, it may well have been seen or copied by someone.

Video sharing sites

Sites such as YouTube are a potential privacy risk. For example, when you upload a video to a video sharing website you are, in effect, making it available for people to watch forever. This is because online videos are so easy to copy. So even if you later delete a video from the site you uploaded it to, there is a chance that it might reappear on another site because someone else copied it.

Advice to pass onto your children about video sharing

- When you record a video be aware of what else is in the scene. Watch for stuff in the background like posters, photos, clothes, signs and cars. These objects might give away your identity or your location.

- Respect the privacy of others. If you're recording a video in a public place, ask permission before including bystanders. Never video children without the permission of their parents.
- Feel free to express yourself on your videos but don't be nasty. You can be held legally responsible if you slander, libel or defame someone.
- Read and stick to the terms of use of video sharing sites. Most forbid sexually explicit material, violence, and videos that are harassing, defamatory, obscene, libelous, hateful, or violate the privacy of other people. They also prohibit the unauthorised use of copyrighted material such as TV programmes and music.

Identity theft

Identity theft is a phrase that we hear a lot these days. But what is it? Here is a formal definition:

"The crime of obtaining the personal or financial information of another person for the purpose of assuming that person's name to make purchases or to commit a crime."

Identity theft is the fastest-growing online crime. Identity thieves often use the Internet to carry out their work.

What identity thieves want

Put simply, they want to be able to pretend to be you.
By impersonating you, they can:

- buy things using your debit or credit cards;
- take money out of your bank account; and
- commit crimes in your name.

Personal information that is valuable to an identity thief

Your name and address

- This has value to an identity thief, but your name and address alone is not normally enough to do anything with.

Your telephone number

- A listed phone number is a residential number which is published in a phone book. A listed phone number is valuable to an identity thief because, with it, they can also obtain an address. An unlisted phone number is not of much use to an identity thief.

Your credit and debit card details

- It goes without saying that these details are extremely valuable to an identity thief.
- So only ever provide your card details when you are buying from a secure website. Never store these details on your computer – for example, written down within a Word document saved on your computer.

Your driving licence number

- This is potentially very valuable to an identity thief so never give it out online.

Your birth date

- Your date of birth is potentially very valuable to a thief. Provide a fake birth date if a website you really want to use asks for it.

National Insurance or NHS number

- Never give this number out online and don't ever provide a fake one either.

The answers to secret questions

- Websites sometimes ask you to provide the answer to a secret question as part of their registration process. They do this so that, for example, you can automatically reset your password if you ever forget it. They ask you the secret to validate that the person making the request is really you. Your mother's maiden name is a commonly asked – for secret question. So never unintentionally reveal the answers to any secret questions you have been asked for on other websites.

How identity thieves can get hold of the information they need to commit their crimes

Identity thieves use a variety of methods. Sometimes they use software such as computer viruses, trojan horses and worms to infect computers. These bits of software then search the computers they infect looking for personal information they can use to steal the victim's identity.

Another method they use is to physically get access to a computer. So always keep your computer safe when you're out and about with it. As mentioned earlier, a privacy software program can safeguard the private information on your computer in the event that it is lost or stolen.

Worryingly, sometimes all identity thieves have to do is to obtain information that someone has published about themselves on a website such as Facebook. Also they sometimes operate websites that trick people into supplying information about themselves.

What to do if you're worried

Make sure that your bank details or credit or debit cards have not been stolen by:

- always checking your bank and credit card statements; and
- checking your credit rating regularly with a credit reference agency.

If you suspect that someone has stolen your bank or card details then you should contact your bank or credit card company immediately.

In the UK, if an organisation loses your personal information and you end up suffering financial damage as a consequence you are entitled to compensation under section 13 of the Data Protection Act. If you fail to get compensation, you also have the right to go to court to retrieve the money you've lost.

Buy a shredder and use it to dispose of any bits of paper that contain personal details. Keep any documents with personal information in a safe place and shred them when you have no further use for them.

There is UK website where you can go for help. Identity Theft (www.identity-theft.org.uk) is run by a group of public and private sector bodies including the Home Office.

DANGER 5

Cyberbullying

Cyberbullying is using the Internet or a mobile phone to threaten, tease or abuse someone. It's against the law and, sadly, it's become quite common.

Cyberbullies use email. Instant Messaging (IM), chat rooms, online games and social networking websites to reach their victims.

It's a serious matter and is a form of emotional abuse. Cyberbullying can leave a victim feeling vulnerable, upset, scared, lonely, stressed and feeling that there's no way out.

The size of the problem

According to a survey published in September 2006 by ABC News in the USA:

- 42% of children have been cyberbullied;
- 25% have been bullied in this way more than once;
- over a third of children have been threatened; and
- 21% of children have received nasty or threatening emails or other messages.

What makes it worse is that most victims don't tell anyone. Almost 6 out of 10 of children have not told their parents or an adult about something nasty or hurtful that happened to them while they were online.

Examples of cyberbullying

Here are some examples of what could be regarded as cyberbullying.

- Sending a person an email which contains an abusive message, unsuitable images or a computer virus.

- Creating a fake profile for a person on a social networking website such as Facebook.
- Leaving an abusive message on a person's Facebook page.
- Sending an abusive text message.

Why do Cyberbullies do what they do?

There is no one answer. Common reasons why cyberbullies do what they do include:

- jealousy or revenge;
- thinking it makes them look cool or hard; and
- a form of entertainment.

Often cyberbullies think they're less likely to get caught if they bully using a mobile phone or the Internet. But cyberbullies cannot remain anonymous. Ultimately they can still be tracked down even if they use a false name or email address.

What to do if you're worried

Advice to pass onto your children

- Never reply to bullying messages. Some kind of a response is exactly what the bully wants. They want to know that they've got their victim worried.
- Tell someone if you're being bullied. Tell an adult you know and trust.
- If the cyberbullying is being carried out over the Internet then you should report the incident to your Internet Service Provider (ISP).

- If the cyberbullying is being carried out via a mobile then you should report the incident to your mobile network provider.
- Tell the police if the cyberbullying becomes very bad.
- Keep the bullying messages as they might be required as evidence in the future.
- Don't take on the bully yourself. Do not retaliate as you might be thought of as a bully yourself in the future.
- Change all your details if you're being bullied. For example, get a new email address and delete your Facebook profile.
- If you come across someone being bullied, don't get involved in the bullying yourself. Even if you're not a ringleader and targeting someone specifically yourself, you can easily be part of the problem by adding to what's already happened by, for example, forwarding on something that's been sent to you.
- If you do notice bullying taking place on an Instant Messenging system, in a chatroom or on a social networking site report the incident to the operators of the website or service.

Happy slapping

Happy slapping is a very unpleasant type of cyberbullying. It is where someone physically attacks an unsuspecting victim, the incident is filmed by an accomplice and the clip is then published on the Internet.

Happy slapping is a crime. In March 2008 a teenage girl who filmed the fatal beating of a man on her mobile phone was sentenced to two years' detention. This was the first prosecution of its kind in the UK

She had pleaded guilty at Leeds Crown Court in February 2008 to aiding and abetting the manslaughter of Gavin Waterhouse. Mark Masters and Sean Thompson were sentenced to seven and six years respectively after admitting to Mr Waterhouse's manslaughter.

Just before the attack, the girl was handed a mobile phone by one of the attackers and told to "video this." She then approached Gavin Waterhouse, asked for money, and recorded the attack.

Useful links

The Anti-bullying Network – **www.antibullying.net**

Bullying UK – **www.bullying.co.uk**

DANGER 6

Technology addiction

Be warned

Many teenagers are obsessed by the Internet and video games. And it's not just children. The estimate is that two million people a day in the UK spend an hour or more during office time on Facebook.

Studies are finding that technology addiction is a different aspect of the same problem as other addictions such as drugs and gambling. Researchers are also discovering that some people can dabble in potentially addictive pastimes but others get hit by it the first time they use it.

Technologies such as the Internet are continually tempting us. Because so many of the things that you can do online are fun or useful, they are placing ever greater demands on our self-control.

At a basic level, addiction is when the brain's reward system gets taken over. The reward system is the part of the brain that motivates us to do things that ensure that we survive. Like eating and drinking, for example. When we do something that helps us survive this part of the brain releases a chemical called dopamine which makes us feel good.

The reward system is wired into the part of our brain that stores our memories. This means that a note is made in our memory whenever we do something that makes us feel good. In turn, the circuitry in the motor cortex is strengthened. This is the part of our brain that controls our behaviours.

When someone is addicted to something, they do it to excess. This loads the brain with too much dopamine. The reward system then writes really powerful memories related to the activity and that lead to the dopamine rush. This then hotwires the muscle actions needed to carry out the action, which is what the addict then does. This releases more dopamine, which makes the activity seem even more desirable. Before you know it, a cycle has begun and the activity has become an unstoppable craving. Drugs like cocaine and heroin target the reward system and produce massive amounts of dopamine.

We humans are a species that evolved in scarcity. This means that if something is good we have a tendency to want more of it.

Why are some people predisposed to addictive behaviours? Circumstances play a part. People who have underprivileged lives or who are depressed are naturally inclined to seek out pleasure wherever they can.

The prefrontal cortex is the part of the brain responsible for decision-making and forming judgments. It is not yet fully developed in adolescents. This is one reason why teenagers are not good at assessing risk and why they are more likely than adults to take drugs.

It is estimated that 40–60% of our susceptibility to addictive behaviours is preprogrammed from birth. Some people have a deficiency of dopamine receptors in their brain. To compensate for this they can be led to do things that cause dopamine to be produced.

You can become addicted to anything which gives you pleasure. The most addictive online experiences and games are the ones that offer the most enticing reward structures. This includes games where you can get a sense of achievement by completing a task, getting to a new level or expanding a virtual empire. It can also be social situations where you receive praise.

How to spot technology addiction

People use computers so much these days that sometimes it can be difficult to tell the difference between someone who is highly engaged and someone who is truly addicted.

Signs that could indicate a problem include the following.

- Abnormal sleep patterns, such as:
    - going to sleep later than usual and waking later
    - feeling tired in the morning.
- Irritability when not using the computer or gadget.
- Preoccupation with the computer or gadget.
- Becoming angry if told to stop using it.
- Hiding evidence of usage – for example, hiding receipts for video game purchases.
- Hiding evidence of online activities – for example, deleting files on the computer or using encryption software.
- Secretly using the computer or gadget.
- Being defensive when confronted.
- Nightmares or dreams about gaming or computer use.
- Dropping out of social groups and becoming isolated.
- Spending an ever-increasing number of hours online or using the gadget.
- Symptoms of depression which include being in a depressed mood most of the day, taking less of an interest in activities along with insomnia, fatigue, feelings of worthlessness and being less able to think or concentrate.

- Giving up social, work or recreational activities in order to spend time on the Internet or using the gadget.
- Giving the Internet or the gadget more importance in life than is warranted.
- Defending their right to use the computer or gadget as much as they want.

How big is the problem?

No formal studies have been published but a Harris Interactive poll released in April 2007 found that:

- 8.5% of youth gamers in the United States could be "classified as pathological or clinically 'addicted' to playing video games"

A British survey in November 2006 found that 12% of video games players exhibit addictive behaviours.

Video game overuse is believed to be more of a problem in Asia. A governmental survey in South Korea estimated that 2.4% of South Koreans aged 9 to 39 are addicts. It found that 10.2% more are borderline cases.

Some experts reckon that up to 10% of all online Americans are addicted to the Internet.

Children are more vulnerable to addiction than adults. It seems they can be very easily hooked into online games and pornography. Most worryingly, the younger they are, the more vulnerable they are.

In the USA the problem has got to the point where the American Psychiatric Association has actually defined a medical condition they call Internet Addiction Disorder.

Some kids spend between six and twenty hours a day sat in front of the computer.

A 2005 survey by the Entertainment Software Association found that "video game overuse" was more common in players of games which are known as MMORPGs. This stands for Massively Multiplayer Online Role-Playing Games. Ultima Online is an example of just such a game.

An expert in this field, Dr Maressa Orzack of McLean Hospital in Massachusetts estimates that 40% of the 8.5 million players of the MMORPG game World of Warcraft are addicted to it.

Males are most at risk

A 2008 Study by Stanford University School of Medicine suggests that in video games when the game concept revolves around territorial control, addiction in men may be more common than women.

The researchers have shown that the part of the brain that generates rewarding feelings is more activated in men than women during video-game play.

Built-in addiction

Addictive games tempt players with complex systems of goals and achievements. EverQuest, for example, gets players to take part in activities where they can develop their characters from one level to the next. Players can find themselves wrapped up in the game for hours as they struggle to gain one more skill or weapon. Each goal leads to another goal, and there are critical choices to be made along the way. Players end up investing a lot of time and thought into developing a character. So they often feel like they've wasted their time unless they reach the next goal with their character.

Possible causes

Children may overuse the Internet or video games if they're bored. Sometimes they do it to escape from their problems. Many children who have a problem mixing with other kids turn to computers and the Internet as a source of entertainment and social contact.

Many online games addicts are lonely and have never felt like they belonged. They get a sense of belonging through the games. Most online games include chat rooms which allow players to chat with each other in the name of the characters they represent.

It's more than just fun that users get. Many video games satisfy basic psychological needs. Often people continue to play because of the rewards they get, the freedom and sense of escapism they enjoy, and the social connection they get from mixing with other players.

Addiction can be caused by psychological problems such as antisocial disorder, depression, and phobias such as social phobia.

Many addicts want a way to escape reality. They find that they can create a whole new persona on an online game. They feel that they can live their life through their make-believe online personality. Because they have new friends and perhaps even a sense of power and control, they can end up preferring their fantasy life to their real life.

Treatment centres

Some countries, like South Korea, have responded to the perceived threat of video game addiction by opening treatment centres. The Chinese government operates several clinics to treat those addicted to online games, chatting and web surfing.

What to do if you're worried

- Do not 'cut the cord'. Removing access to the computer or the gadget completely in one swoop can lead to worse outcomes. It can lead to drug use or depression.
- Some experts advocate a 'retreat' or rehab-like setting for a minimum of 2 weeks.
- Put the computer in a public place such as the living room or the kitchen so that they will find it more difficult to spend hours online.
- Get the child to acknowledge that they have a problem and that their behaviour is not helping them.
- As with other types of addiction, try to find out what the difficulty is that is at the root of things. Perhaps what they're doing is serving as an escape from an everyday life problem. If another problem is the root cause and the addiction has become an escape, work together to create a plan to sort that problem out.
- Then get them to take steps to resolve the addiction itself. A gradual decline in use is best until a sensible amount of time is reached. Be patient and understanding. Remember that this is a habit the person has gotten into and it can be difficult breaking a habit. So if, for example, they are used to coming in straight from school and logging on, get them into the habit of doing something else first.
- If the Internet is the problem, you could get them to set goals for themselves for gradually reducing the hours they spend online. Also get them to set targets for what they want to accomplish each time they go online so that they do not log on and surf aimlessly.

- Teach them how to manage their urge to go online. So each time they feel that strong urge, get them to sit quietly and experience the urge feeling. If they do that, the urge will eventually pass and they will feel fine again. Eventually they will form a new habit of responding to the urge.
- Visit the website www.netaddiction.com for more information and advice.

DANGER 7

Scams and commercial exploitation

Be warned

Children and teenagers are more likely than adults to fall victim to deception and con tricks. Part of the reason for this is biological. The part of the brain that helps us make decisions is still developing in children and young people. This means that they're not as good as adults at spotting scams and making good decisions.

Competitions

Children love online competitions. The Internet is awash with them. Often the organisers deliberately make their contests look appealing to children. For example, they make them quick and easy to enter.

While some competitions are obviously genuine, many are not. Often the aim for the organisers of these hoax contests is simply to collect personal information so that they can later bombard the entrants with advertising.

Online shopping

Online shopping seems so natural to children and young people because they've grown up with it. In the USA, children already do about 15% of all their spending on the Internet.

A lot of companies specifically target their marketing at teenagers. To persuade them to buy, companies use tactics that children go for like web pages with lots of colour, animation, interactivity plus low prices.

Scams

The Internet has given a new lease of life to age-old con tricks such as pyramid schemes and chain letters. The Internet makes it very easy for con artists to rip people off, hide and move on if necessary. The scams take many forms. For example, emails making promises of easy money and free gifts are quite common.

Phishing

A phishing email is one which appears to come from your bank or another financial organisation. There is normally a link in the email. When you click on it you are taken to a website. It will look like the actual website of the bank or financial organisation. You'll be asked to enter your bank account number and password. If you do, the fraudsters will then have all they need to access your actual online bank account.

Be aware that a legitimate bank will never ask you to provide your personal details such as your account number or online banking password in this way.

So never click on the link contained in a phishing email. Report the incident to your actual bank straightaway.

What to do if you're worried

- Get your child to check with you first before they enter any kind of online competition.
- Check the company behind the competition is reputable and is bona fide. It is very easy to build a fake website so look out for impostors. Install www.siteadvisor.com. It's free software that tells you how safe websites are.
- Read the competition rules and terms and conditions very carefully. Make sure that the company organising the competition will not pass on your details to other companies.
- When online, make sure your children are more cynical and treat things they come across as suspicious unless they have evidence to prove otherwise.

- Never let your kids buy anything unless you are there. Never leave your credit cards, debit cards or the statements lying around the house.
- Never give your credit or debit card number to your children to type into a website. When it comes to that stage in the purchase process, get them to call you over so that you enter the details.
- Be wary of buying from companies that do not have a postal address or a telephone contact number on their site.
- Tell your children not to download games or software without your permission.
- Don't trust a website just because it looks professional. These days it's relatively easy and inexpensive to create, register, and promote a website.

DANGER 8

Malware

There are a number of ways in which your computer can get damaged. Malware is the general name given to the many types of software that can get onto your computer which are hostile, intrusive, or annoying.

Examples are:

- viruses;
- worms;
- trojan horses;
- rootkits;
- spyware; and
- adware.

According to the Internet Security software company, F-Secure:

"As much malware was produced in 2007 as in the previous 20 years altogether."

Viruses and worms

The best-known types of malware are viruses and worms. They get their name from the way in which they spread across computers connected to the Internet.

- Worms spread and infect computers automatically. So if a worm gets into your computer, it will harm it immediately. Worms can infect a computer by, for example, taking advantage of a security weakness in software on the victim's computer.

- A virus can only infect a computer if a certain action is taken. For example, if a virus is sent to your computer in the form of a file attachment to an email, the virus will only go ahead and infect your computer if you open up the email attachment. Hundreds of new viruses are produced every week. The main way they spread is via emails.

Worms and viruses are designed to cause particular types of damage. Some will delete files from your computer. Others will get hold of personal information that's stored on your computer and send it to the creators of the virus or worm.

Trojan horses

A trojan horse is similar to a virus or a worm in that it is a malicious software program. The difference is that it gets into your computer by being hidden inside or disguised as something else such as a useful software program.

Spyware

Spyware is a type of software program that secretly gathers information about you. For example, a spyware program might sit in the background on your computer and note the websites you visit. It might then use this information to display particular advertisements that relate to the kind of websites you visit. This type of spyware is known as adware.

Some spyware programs install what is called a key logger onto your computer. What this does is to record the information you enter into websites such as email addresses, website passwords and even credit card numbers. It then sends this information back to the creator of the spyware program. Another type of spyware is a browser hijacker. What this does is to take over your browser and it then sends you to websites of its choosing such as online shops or search engines.

Very worryingly, stalkers and paedophiles are increasingly using spyware to monitor their targets.

Rootkits

The producers of malware don't want their software to be found. What a rootkit does is to hide the malware by changing the operating system of the computer. This makes the malware very difficult to find and remove.

In the early days, malware programs were mainly created as acts of vandalism or as pranks. Things have changed and nowadays they are mainly created with profit in mind. Many programs are created by criminal gangs. The malware developers can make money by getting hold of your credit card details or by getting you to buy from the websites they send you to.

Spam

Spam is the Internet equivalent of junk mail. It is the word used to describe email you did not ask for that is sent by people or companies you don't know.

These days most spam is sent by unscrupulous businesses and people. Some emails are sent by companies trying to sell you something whilst other spam contains offensive material. Some companies use unsolicited email to promote legitimate products, while others use it for scams. The Federal Trade Commission in the USA recently conducted a study and found that most spam is fraudulent.

You can open yourself up to receiving spam unintentionally. And once you've opened the floodgates it can pour into your email inbox at an alarming rate. So never open and never reply to spam. This is because spammers often put tiny bits of programming code into emails called beacons. Whenever you open an email containing this code you end up telling the spammers that your email account is live. Because they then know that, you will then receive more and more spam from them. Plus they'll tell their spamming friends and you'll get junk from them too. Also, never click on any links contained within spam emails.

You can reduce the amount you receive. But because of the sheer volume of spam in circulation, you can probably never eliminate receiving it completely.

Anti-spam software

Anti-spam software examines your emails. It screens out ones that it thinks are spam. For example, it will filter out emails sent from particular email addresses or locations that are well-known for being originators of spam. It will also treat emails that contain particular word patterns as spam.

Anti-spam software is not perfect, however. Some legitimate emails will be screened out and sent to your spam folder. Also some spam will inevitably slip through the net and find its way into your inbox.

Spim

Spam sent via Instant Messaging systems is called spim. It is a growing problem.

Almost all spim messages take the form of short one-liners with links to websites. It is estimated that:

- 70% of spim messages are pornographic;
- 12% promote get-rich-quick schemes; and
- 9% attempt to sell products.

It goes without saying that you should never click on a link on a spim message.

Mobile phone viruses

Unfortunately viruses no longer simply affect computers. The first ever virus capable of spreading between mobile phones, Cabir, was discovered in 2004.

Windows Operating System and browser problems

Email is not the only way that viruses can get into your computer. They can also get in because of flaws in operating systems such as Windows.

Vulnerabilities can also exist with web browsers such as Internet Explorer. Hackers and malware can exploit these defects and get viruses in through these 'back door' routes.

You can solve the problem by always making sure that the versions of your operating system and browser are up-to-date. The company that produces Windows, Microsoft, creates updates called patches every time they discover a defect in Windows or Explorer. Microsoft never distributes these patches by email. So if you ever get an email which says that it contains a security patch then you should delete it. It will almost certainly be malware.

Hackers

Your computer is at risk from attack by hackers any time that you are on the Internet. This is particularly true if you have a broadband Internet connection.

This is because when you are online your computer has a number, called an IP address, which can be seen by other people who have the required technical knowledge. Using it they can get into your computer without you knowing.

You can protect yourself against such attacks with what is called a firewall. A firewall, in effect, stands guard at the entrance to your computer and stops hackers getting in.

You can have firewalls which are pieces of equipment or, more commonly for home users, there are software firewall programs.

Other ways of protecting your computer

Here are some other ways of protecting your computer.

- Even if you've got a firewall and anti-spyware software it's still a good idea to 'password protect' or encrypt (that is, scramble) files on your computer that contain confidential information, such as private correspondence or credit card details.

Backups

You should do regular backups of the important files on your computer. This is in case they get deleted by accident or in case your computer gets damaged by a virus and cannot be switched on again.

There are many ways of doing a backup such as saving files onto CDs. But one of the best ways is to do it online. This means that your files are saved outside your home, which is doubly safe. There are many companies that provide this kind of service such as Carbonite (www.carbonite.com).

DANGER 8

Breaking the law

Be warned

Children and teenagers can break the law while using the Internet without realising it.

The main ones to be aware of are the laws of:

- copyright;
- libel; and
- obscenity.

Other crimes include:

- hacking;
- invading the privacy of other people; and
- distributing computer viruses.

This issue shouldn't be taken lightly. Action is taken by the authorities in relation to illegal acts as regards these issues. There have been cases of the police and schools taking action against teenagers because of things they've done and comments they've made in emails, in chat rooms and on websites such as Facebook.

Copyright

Copyright legislation applies to a wide range of creative work. Examples include words, music, video, software and pictures. One of the problems is that the Internet makes it very easy to create and distribute illegal copies of copyrighted material.

Napster

The most famous example of copyright infringement was the Napster website. It simplified the process of sharing and downloading free music over the Internet. Eventually it was shut down. Other less famous sites still exist that offer the same service.

Libel

This is where you publish a public statement about someone that is derogatory and untrue. People who make libelous comments on the Internet can, in theory, be sued in the same way that newspapers, magazines and other forms of media can. The law applies to emails, the content of websites, conversations in chat rooms, and postings to message boards.

Obscenity

If you publish something obscene on the web you can be breaking the law. It can also be an offence to have obscene material on your computer. This is the case even if you don't know you have it, or if you came across it by accident.

Behave with netiquette

Research is revealing that people sometimes behave on the Internet in ways that they would not do if they were face-to-face with people.

The fact that people can remain anonymous on the Internet is part of the reason why this happens. They don't have to deal with the consequences of what they say. They cannot see the people they are communicating with. This means that they cannot adjust what they're saying based on the reactions of the people they are talking to.

This situation is complicated when it comes to children and young people. This is because they're still learning the social rules of life. They're also still developing their critical evaluation skills.

Whenever you communicate with someone using the Internet it is important to do so with respect. When you are online all you see is a computer screen and sometimes it is easy to forget that there is a real person with feelings at the other end of what you say. When we communicate with someone face-to-face we pick up things like facial expressions, gestures, and tone of voice. Online you don't have those cues so it can be easy to misinterpret things.

It's important to remember that Internet forms of communication such as email and messages posted on Facebook are stored.
So comments can come back to haunt you.

It is important to behave well and in accordance with the rules of Internet etiquette – or netiquette as it is known. See www.netmanners.com for more information Internet etiquette.

Here are the three main rules of Internet etiquette.

- Remember that there is always a person at the other end of what you write.
- Don't write in capital letters. It is the Internet equivalent of shouting.
- Don't swear. Comments can't be taken back.

What to do if you're worried

Advice you can offer your children

- Do not download anything from the Internet if you are not sure if it is free of copyright.
- Do not write anything malicious or untruthful over the Internet.
- Behave in accordance with netiquette.

DANGER 10

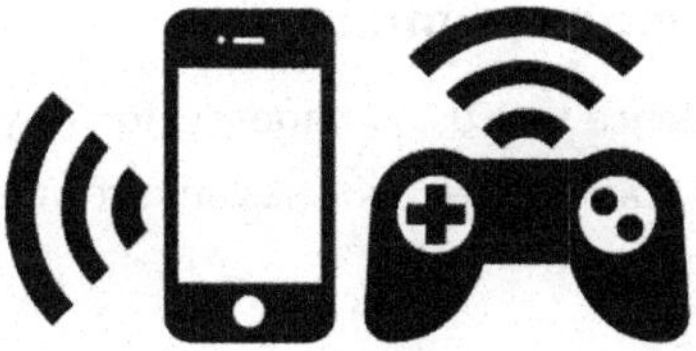

Gadgets

Mobile phones

Radiation from mobile phones

There is growing evidence that using handsets for 10 years or more can double the risk of brain cancer. Cancers can take at least a decade to develop.

In 2008, the French government warned against the use of mobile phones, especially by children. The German government has issued similar advice in the past.

A recent review of more than a hundred studies on the effects of mobile phones by top neurosurgeon Professor Khurana lead him to conclude:

"... there is a significant and increasing body of evidence for a link between mobile phone usage and certain brain tumours."

Children may be more at risk. Research published by the Independent Experts Group on Mobile Phones (IEGMP) suggests that children may be more vulnerable to health risks from mobile phone use. This is because their nervous systems are still developing.

The IEGMP bases its statement on the fact that children have smaller heads, thinner skulls, and higher tissue conductivity than adults. This means that they may absorb more energy from a mobile phone than adults.

Expensive mobile phone bills

Mobile phone scams are not uncommon. Here are some common examples.

- You get a text message saying that you have won some

kind of prize. When you call the number given to claim your prize, you are forced to listen to a long message. At the end of the message you either find that there is no prize after all, or that there is a prize but that it has all kinds of conditions attached. When you get your bill at the end of the month you find that the call was to a very expensive premium rate number.

- You ring a joke line number for a small amount of money and then later find that you have signed up to receive a new joke on a regular basis at, say, 50p a time.
- A "Call this number urgently" message asking you to ring a number. You end up listening to a sales pitch of some kind for something you don't want – at a premium rate call charge.

Bluetooth phones

Bluetooth is the name for a type of wireless technology. It allows electronic gadgets such as phones and computers to communicate with each other over short distances. It is an alternative to using cables to transfer stuff like photos or contact details between devices.

The Bluetooth setting can normally be switched on or off as required.

Gadgets fitted with Bluetooth pose privacy and safety risks.

Bluesnarfing is where an attacker is able to get into their victim's mobile phone using Bluetooth and take the data from it. This can include contacts, appointments and even photos. The attacker can also send text messages and make telephone calls via the victim's phone.

A bluesnarfing attack can take place without the victim knowing it has happened. In recent years handset manufacturers have begun to fix the problem in newer phones.

Bluejacking is where someone sends out unwanted text messages to people nearby who also have a Bluetooth phone. Any phones with Bluetooth that are within range can pick up these messages.

Bluejacking is popular with children and teenagers. Bluejacking can be used in a harmless and fun way but also can be used as a form of nuisance calling and bullying.

Advice to pass onto children and teenagers

- Be cautious about who you give your mobile phone number to.
- Never respond to text messages that say you have won a competition or anything similar.
- Pairing is when two Bluetooth devices have been set up to communicate with each other. So regularly check the pairings on your mobile phone and other Bluetooth gadgets. Remove any unwanted ones.
- When you're in a public place either switch Bluetooth off on your mobile phone or set it to 'non-discoverable' so that it'll be invisible to potential attackers.
- Don't ever lend your phone to anyone you do not trust. This is because they could set up a pairing between one of their devices and your phone.
- Used mobile phones can still have pairing information on them. So the thing to do is to perform what is known as a 'full factory reset'. This clears all the settings back to when the phone was first manufactured.

Video games

Be warned

There are a number of potential benefits for children and young people from playing video games. They include cognitive improvements and having fun.

However, if a child of yours plays video games you'll know what it can do to them in a negative sense. Some games can cause them to get upset or frustrated. Also, some video games can arouse and stimulate them to such an extent that they exhibit stress-like symptoms. It can also be difficult getting them to come off the games at times.

The content of some video games can be unsuitable for children and teenagers. Themes that are sometimes depicted include:

- graphic violence;
- sexual scenes;
- advergaming (a form of advertising in games);
- consumption of drugs and alcohol;
- propaganda; and
- bad language.

Other reasons for concern include the following issues.

- Some children and young people can end up becoming addicted to video games. In 2011 in the UK, a 20-year old young man called Chris Staniforth was killed by a blood clot caused by playing his Xbox for up to 12 hours at a time.
- There is a relationship between playing violent video games and aggressive behaviour. But there is no scientific evidence yet that one causes the other.

- Young children are less able to distinguish between fact and fiction. This means that video games are more likely to affect their perceptions and expectations of the real world.
- There is some evidence that exposure to pornography and the excessive use of video games can cause emotional harm.

Only "17% of surveyed children say their parents check the ratings on the video games they buy."

The Kaiser Family Foundation

What to do if you're worried

- Always check the rating for video games. Use the ratings as a guide but do not only rely on them. Make your own mind up based on your child. Consider your child's personality, maturity and abilities.
- Also when considering whether a game is suitable for your child:
    - speak to older children and other parents;
    - rent before purchasing;
    - read game reviews;
    - try out demos of the game online or in a store where the game is sold.
- Look closely at the box the game comes in. Most have screen shots of the game on the back of the box showing typical scenes from the game.
- Play video games with your children. Playing or observing helps you understand what they get from the game.

- Consider the option of using the parental controls feature if you're worried. Newer video game systems allow parents to restrict specific game content by rating.
- Be cautious with online-enabled games. Many popular games can be played with friends (and strangers) over the Internet.
- Be aware of 'mods' that can change a game. These are downloadable bits of software that can alter game content and the game's age-appropriateness. Some mods can contain viruses or spyware, making them dangerous.

Appendices

APPENDIX 1: MORE INFORMATION

Visit our Internet Dangers site

InternetDangers
SHOWING YOU HOW TO SURF SAFELY

You'll find:

Up-to-date articles on the latest Internet and technology dangers

Videos which show you in a simple, step-by-step way how to do some of the things recommended in this book

www.internetdangers.com

Join our campaign

Protechtion

We have started a crusade called Protechtion which is calling on everyone to do what they can to make technology safer for children, young people and vulnerable adults.

Protechtion also:
- promotes the positive uses of the Internet and technology;
- generates ideas to solve the problems posed by the Internet and technology dangers;
- educates parents, children, young people and vulnerable adults about the dangers; and
- provides services which help people who have fallen victim to the dangers.

Go to www.protechtion.org.uk for more information, to make a donation or to sign up to our campaign.

APPENDIX 2: USEFUL LINKS

UK Organisations

The Child Exploitation and Online Protection Centre (CEOP) work to stop child abuse on the Internet. Parents and young people can use this site to report abuse or attempted abuse.
www.ceop.police.uk

ThinkUknow is the Child Exploitation and Online Protection (CEOP) Centre's website for children, which provides them with information on internet safety.
www.thinkuknow.co.uk

The Internet Watch Foundation is the UK's hotline for reporting illegal content on the Internet.
www.iwf.org.uk

International Organisations

Childnet International works in partnership with others around the world to help make the Internet a great place and a safe place for children.
www.childnet-int.org

Wired Safety was the world's first Internet safety and help group.
www.wiredsafety.org

Insafe is a European network of Awareness Centres promoting safe, responsible use of the Internet and mobile devices to young people.
www.saferinternet.org

APPENDIX 3: JARGON BUSTER

Attachment: a computer file that is sent from one person to another attached to an email. It may be a Microsoft Word file or a photo, for example.

Broadband: a fast, 'always-on' connection to the Internet.

Browser: this is a piece of software which allows you to look at websites. Microsoft Explorer is a browser.

Chat room: this is a place on the Internet where people can talk to each other there and then by typing messages into their computer or mobile phone.

Download: this means to transfer information and files (software, music, etc.) from a website to your computer.

Email (electronic mail): this is a facility whereby you can type and send messages electronically over the Internet to another person.

Email address: this is the email equivalent of a postal address – an example of an email address is steve@internetdangers.com

Favourites: this is a feature of the Explorer browser that allows you to store website addresses that you don't want to forget.

Filter: a piece of software that allows you to block out websites that contain certain material such as pornography.

Firewalls: this is either software or equipment that stops people gaining access to your computer when you are on the Internet.

Instant Messaging: this is a facility whereby people can have a live text conversation with each other by typing messages.

ISP (Internet Service Provider): this is a company that provides people and businesses with access to the Internet. Examples include BT, Sky and Virgin Media.

MMS (multi-media messaging): this is a service whereby you can send messages between mobile phones – you can send simple text messages or even photographs, video or audio.

Modem: this is the part of your computer (or it can even be a separate piece of equipment) that allows your computer to connect to the Internet.

Moderated chat room: this is a chat room where the conversations that take place are monitored and supervised either by a person or a piece of technology.

Newsgroups: sometimes also known as groups, these are message boards where people post messages to others about particular topics.

Online: this is a term which means being on the Internet. When you are not online you are said to be offline.

Picture messaging: some mobile phones now include an in-built still or video camera. When you use them to take a picture and then send that picture to someone else who has a similar phone you are sending a picture message.

Profile: some chat rooms ask users to provide information about themselves such as name, age and hobbies. This is called their profile.

SMS: this is short for Short Messaging Service and means sending a text message to a mobile phone (it is sometimes also known as texting).

URL: see under Website Address.

Website Address: (sometimes also known as a URL or domain name) this is what you type into the browser in order to be taken to a website.

Webcams: these are small cameras that can be used to send video images over the Internet.

Whispering: this is the term for sending a private message to someone while in a chat room. As in the real world, it is safer to stay in the public area.

APPENDIX 4: COMMON ABBREVIATIONS USED IN CHAT ROOMS AND IN TEXTING

2L8	Too late
2U2	To you too
4GM	Forgive me
4RL?	For real?
AAMOF	As a matter of fact
AAYF	As always, your friend
AFAIK	As far as I know
AFK	Away from keyboard
AKA	Also known as
ASAP	As soon as possible
ASL	Age, sex, location?
ASLP	Age, sex, location, picture?
ATM	At the moment
ATYS	Anything you say
AWA	As well as
B4	Before
B4N	Bye for now
BAC	Back at computer
BAK	Back at keyboard
BBIAB	Be back in a bit
BBL	Be back later
BBS	Be back soon
BCNU	Be seeing you
BD	Big deal
BFD	Big freaking deal
BF	Boyfriend
BFN	Bye for now
BC	Be cool
B/C	Because

BIL	Brother in law
BME	Based on my experience
BOT	Back on topic
BRH	Be right here
BRB	Be right back
BTDT	Been there, done that
BTW	By the way
BYTM	Better you than me
CMIIW	Correct me if I'm wrong
CU	See you
CUL	Catch you later
CUS	See you soon
CUL8R	See you later
CWOT	Complete waste of time
CYA	See you
CYL	Catch you later
DBEYR	Don't believe everything you read
DHYB	Don't hold your breath
DIIK	Darned if I know
DIY	Do it yourself
DQYDJ	Don't quit your day job
EAK	Eating at keyboard
EG	Evil grin
EOD	End of discussion
EOL	End of lecture
EOR	End of rant
F	Female
F2F	Face to face
FCOL	For crying out loud
FIL	Father in law
FITB	Fill in the blanks
FNB	Football and beer
FOCL	Falling off the chair laughing

FOFL	Falling on the floor laughing
FWIW	For what it's worth
FYA	For your amusement
FYI	For your information
G	Grin
G2G	Gotta go
GA	Go ahead
GA	Good afternoon
GAL	Get a life
GAS	Greetings and salutations
GBH	Great Big Hug
GE	Good evening
GF	Girlfriend
GFN	Gone for now
GG	Good game
GI	Good idea
GICBTS	Gosh, I can't believe that stuff!
GICNBY	Gosh, I cannot believe you!
GIWISI	Gee, I wish I said it
GJ	Good job
GL	Good luck
GM	Good morning
GM	Good move/match
GMTA	Great minds think alike
GN	Good night
GR8	Great
GTG	Got to go
H	Hug
HB	Hug back
H&K	Hugs and Kisses
HAGD	Have a good day
HAND	Have a nice day
HCIT	How cool is that

HF	Have fun
HH	Ha-ha
HHSF	Ha-ha, so funny
HHVF	Ha-ha, very funny
HO	Hold on
H/O	Hold on
HOAS	Hold on a second
HTH	Hope this helps
IAC	In any case
IAG	It's all good
IAGW	In a good way
IB2D	I beg to differ
IC	I see
IC	In character
IDGI	I don't get it
IDK	I don't know
IDNDT	I did not do that
IIRC	If I remember correctly
IK	I know
IKWUM	I know what you mean
IMAO	In my arrogant opinion
IME	In my experience
IMHO	In my humble opinion
IMHBMAO	In my humble but most accurate opinion
IMNSHO	In my not so humble opinion
INRS	It's not rocket science
IOW	In other words
IRL	In real life
IRSTBO	It really sucks the big one
IS	I'm sorry
ISWYM	I see what you mean
JMHO	Just my humble opinion
JTLYK	Just to let you know

J/K	Just kidding
J/P	Just playing
K	OK
KIR	Keeping it real
KISS	Keep it simple, stupid
KIT	Keep in touch
KWIM	Know what I mean?
KYSOTI	Keep your stick on the ice
L8R	Later
LMK	Let me know
LTR	Long term relationship
LYK	Let you know
LYLAB	Love you like a brother
LYLAS	Love you like a sister
LMAO	Laughing my aoo off
LMBO	Laughing my butt off
LOL	Laugh out loud
LTNS	Long time, no see
LUM	Love you man
M	Male
M8	Mate, a.k.a. friend
ME2	Me too
MIL	Mother in law
MMA	Meet me at ...
MMAMP	Meet me at my place
MOO	My own opinion
MYOB	Mind your own business
N	In
NBD	No big deal
N2M	Not too much
N/C	Not cool
NE1	Anyone
NFW	No freaking way

NLT	No later than
NM	Never mind
NM	Not much
NMH	Not much here
NMJC	Nothing much, just chilling'
NNITO	Not necessarily in that order
NO1	No one
NOTTOMH	Not off the top of my head
NOYB	None of your business
NP	No problem
NRN	No reply necessary
NVM	Never mind
NW	No way
OIC	Oh, I see
OMG	Oh my gosh
OMOHOD	One minute, one hour, one day
ONNA	Oh no, not again
OOC	Out of character
OT	Off topic
OT	Other topic
OTOH	On the other hand
PIMP	Pee in my pants (w/ ROTFL)
PLZ	Please
POS	Parent over shoulder
PPL	People
QT	Cutie
RESQ	Rescue
RFC	Request for comment
RHIP	Rank hath its privileges
ROF	Rolling on the floor
ROFLMAO	Rolling on floor, laughing my aoo off
ROTFL	Rolling on the floor laughing
RTFM	Read the flipping' manual

S2R	Send to receive
S/B	Should be
SCNR	Sorry, could not resist
SK8	Skate
SIL	Sister in law
SLY	Still love you
SOS	Someone Special
SOS	Same old stuff
SOS	Sibling over shoulder
SSDD	Same stuff, different day
STR8	Straight
SWALK	Sweet, with all love, kisses
SWAK	Sealed with a kiss
SWDYWTTA	So what do you want to talk about?
SYSOP	System Operator (chat monitor)
TBC	To be continued
TC	Take care
TC	That's cool
TCO	Taken care of
TGIF	Thank goodness it's Friday
TOH	The other half
THX	Thanks
TNX	Thanks
TIA	Thanks in advance
TMA	Take my advice
TMI	Too much information
TTFN	Ta ta for now
TTYL	Talk to you later
TTYS	Talk to you soon
TTYVS	Talk to you very soon
TWIMC	To whom it may concern
TY	Thank you
TYVM	Thank you very much

U2	You too
UR	You are
UR	Your
URSKTM	You are so kind to me
VBG	Very big grin
W/	With
W2F	Way too funny
W8	Wait
W8AM	Wait a minute
WB	Welcome back
WB	Write back
WC	Who cares
WDMB	Will do my best
WE	Whatever
W/E	Whatever
WNDITWB	We never did it this way before
W/O	Without
WRT	With Regard To
WTF	What the f?
WTG	Way to go!
WWJD	What would Jesus do?
XOXOXO	Hugs and kisses
Y	Why?
YMMV	Your mileage may vary
YRG	You are good!
YVW	You're very welcome
YW	You're welcome
>U!	Screw you!
?	Huh?
?4U	Question for you